STARK LIBRARY FEB - - 2022

BEFORE AND DURING READING ACTIVITIES

Before Reading: *Building Background Knowledge and Vocabulary*

Building background knowledge can help children process new information and build upon what they already know. Before reading a book, it is important to tap into what children already know about the topic. This will help them develop their vocabulary and increase their reading comprehension.

Questions and Activities to Build Background Knowledge:

1. Look at the front cover of the book and read the title. What do you think this book will be about?
2. What do you already know about this topic?
3. Take a book walk and skim the pages. Look at the table of contents, photographs, captions, and bold words. Did these text features give you any information or predictions about what you will read in this book?

Vocabulary: *Vocabulary Is Key to Reading Comprehension*

Use the following directions to prompt a conversation about each word.

- Read the vocabulary words.
- What comes to mind when you see each word?
- What do you think each word means?

Vocabulary Words:
- biology
- ecology
- environmental
- fisheries
- natural history
- pesticide
- successive
- tide pools

During Reading: *Reading for Meaning and Understanding*

To achieve deep comprehension of a book, children are encouraged to use close reading strategies. During reading, it is important to have children stop and make connections. These connections result in deeper analysis and understanding of a book.

Close Reading a Text

During reading, have children stop and talk about the following:

- Any confusing parts
- Any unknown words
- Text to text, text to self, text to world connections
- The main idea in each chapter or heading

Encourage children to use context clues to determine the meaning of any unknown words. These strategies will help children learn to analyze the text more thoroughly as they read.

When you are finished reading this book, turn to the next-to-last page for **Text-Dependent Questions** and an **Extension Activity**.

TABLE OF CONTENTS

A Life in Nature 4
Exploring the Sea 10
Sharing the Ocean 14
Time Line 21
Glossary..22
Index..23
Text-Dependent Questions......................23
Extension Activity...23
About the Author and Illustrator............24

A LIFE IN NATURE

Rachel Carson loved nature and writing. She grew up on a farm. Her mother taught her the names of plants and the calls of animals.

At age eight, Rachel wrote a story about two birds searching for a house. This would just be the start of her interest in nature and writing.

She hoped she would one day see the ocean. "I used to imagine what it would look like, and what the surf sounded like," she said.

Then her father sold off parts of their farm. People built shops in what used to be the farm fields. They changed nature.

Rachel's mother did not have a formal education. She wanted Rachel to get an education. She sold apples and chickens to pay Rachel's college fees. She sold the family dishes.

First Rachel studied English. Then, she met Mary Scott Skinker. Mary ran the **biology** department. She inspired Rachel to study biology.

Mary Scott Skinker studied **natural history**. She believed it was important to save rare plants and animals. She encouraged Rachel's love of nature.

Rachel wanted to stay in school. But she had to support her whole family. She taught college classes and worked in a lab. Rachel's mother and sick father lived with her. Rachel's sister moved in with two young children. Sometimes the family only had apples to eat.

Finally, Rachel had to leave school. She needed a job that paid more.

EXPLORING THE SEA

Government jobs paid well. Rachel took tests that would help her get a government job. The tests were about science topics. She did very well. The U.S. Bureau of **Fisheries** hired her. She was only the second woman they ever hired.

Rachel first saw the ocean during a research trip. She walked along the shore. She waded into **tide pools** and studied the animals there. She fell in love with the sea. Rachel wrote about sea life for radio shows. She called one series "Romance Under the Waters."

Fish and Wildlife Service
The U.S. Bureau of Fisheries became part of the Fish and Wildlife Service. This group manages fish and wildlife. It tries to keep nature healthy. It also helps people enjoy the outdoors.

Rachel wanted everyone to love nature. She wrote articles for newspapers and magazines.

Rachel's articles sounded like poetry. "The edge of the sea is a strange and beautiful place," she wrote. "For no two **successive** days is the shoreline precisely the same. ... Today a little more land may belong to the sea, tomorrow a little less."

Most people thought humans were far more important than animals. Rachel asked people to care for nature too.

SHARING THE OCEAN

Rachel wrote books about the ocean. She said people are only one part of nature. We can change nature. We sometimes make it worse.

"Wildlife ... is dwindling because its home is being destroyed," she wrote. "But the home of the wildlife is also our home."

She won many awards. Some had prize money. She quit her job and moved to an island in Maine to write.

A friend wrote Rachel a letter. She said many birds died after **pesticide** spraying. Rachel knew she had to write about this. She wrote *Silent Spring*.

Deadly Pesticides
Pesticides are chemicals that kill insects. Some pesticides can cause cancer in humans. Fish and wildlife may show changes due to chemical use. Those are clues to the chemical's danger.

This book showed how everything in nature is connected. Once bird song filled the mornings. Then people poisoned insects. Birds ate the insects and the poison. The birds died. Spring went silent. This shows "the web of life—or death—that scientists know as ecology," Rachel wrote.

The book made some people angry. Farmers used pesticides to protect their crops. Companies made money selling pesticides. They did not want to stop. They did not want to believe pesticides were dangerous.

Rachel knew people would be angry. Still, she had to write it. "Knowing what I do, there would be no future peace for me if I kept silent," she wrote.

Silent Spring started the modern **environmental** movement. People realized they had to protect nature. The government passed new laws to protect the earth.

Rachel loved nature. She helped save nature.

TIME LINE

1907: Rachel is born in Springdale, Pennsylvania, on May 27.

1925: Rachel attends Pennsylvania College for Women (now Chatham University).

1929: Rachel graduates from Pennsylvania College for Women.

1932: Rachel completes her master's degree in zoology in from Johns Hopkins University.

1935: Rachel gets a job with the U.S. Bureau of Fisheries.

1941: Rachel publishes her first book, *Under the Sea-Wind*.

1951: Rachel publishes *The Sea Around Us*. It wins awards and is translated into at least 30 languages.

1953: Rachel moves to an island off the coast of Maine to write full time.

1955: Rachel publishes *The Edge of the Sea*.

1962: *Silent Spring* is published. It is also printed in *The New Yorker* magazine over several issues.

1963: The President's Science Advisory Committee issues a report on pesticides. It supports Rachel's warnings.

1964: Rachel dies on April 14 in Silver Spring, Maryland. She is 56.

1965: Rachel's last book, *The Sense of Wonder*, is published.

1970: The Environmental Protection Agency is formed. This agency's mission is to protect human and environmental health.

1972: The pesticide DDT is banned for use in the US. The Clean Water Act is passed.

1973: The Endangered Species Act is passed.

1980: Rachel is awarded the Presidential Medal of Freedom.

GLOSSARY

biology (bye-AH-luh-jee): the science that studies all living things

ecology (i-KAH-luh-jee): the science that studies connections between living things and where they live

environmental (en-VYE-ruhn-MUHNT-uhl): relating to the natural world

fisheries (FISH-uh-reez): businesses that catch or breed fish and other seafood

natural history (NACH-ur-uhl HIS-tur-ee): the science that studies animals, plants, and objects in nature

pesticide (PES-ti-side): a chemical used to kill insects that harm plants

successive (suhk-SES-iv): following one after another

tide pools (tide pools): shallow areas of sea water remaining on the beach once the tide has gone out

INDEX

chemical(s) 16
climate change 19
college 6, 8
Dorothy Freeman 15
government 10, 20
Mary Scott Skinker 6, 7
Silent Spring 16, 17, 20
The U.S. Bureau of Fisheries 10, 11

TEXT-DEPENDENT QUESTIONS

1. How did Rachel's childhood teach her to love nature?
2. When did Rachel discover the beauty of the seashore?
3. How did Rachel's writing teach people about nature?
4. How can pesticides harm nature and people?
5. Why did Rachel write the book *Silent Spring*?

EXTENSION ACTIVITY

An ecosystem is made up of living things and the place they live. Choose an ecosystem to study. It might be a place near you. What plants and animals live there? How do people affect them? Is this ecosystem in danger? If so, how? What would you do to help it?

ABOUT THE AUTHOR

M.M. Eboch also writes books as Chris Eboch. She likes to write about science and history. Her novel The Eyes of Pharaoh is a mystery in ancient Egypt. The Well of Sacrifice is an adventure about the Maya. She lives in New Mexico with her husband and their two ferrets.

ABOUT THE ILLUSTRATOR

Elena Bia was born in a little town in northern Italy, near the Alps. In her free time, she puts her heart into personal comics. She loves walking on the beach and walking through the woods. For her, flowers are the most beautiful form of life.

© 2021 Rourke Educational Media

All rights reserved. No part of this book may be reproduced or utilized in any form or by any means, electronic or mechanical including photocopying, recording, or by any information storage and retrieval system without permission in writing from the publisher.

www.rourkeeducationalmedia.com

Quote sources: Jill Lepore, "The Right Way to Remember Rachel Carson," The New Yorker, March 19, 2018: https://www.newyorker.com/magazine/2018/03/26/the-right-way-to-remember-rachel-carson
Rachel Carson, "The Marginal World," Bookanista, http://bookanista.com/marginal-world/

Edited by: Hailey Scragg
Illustrated by: Elena Bia
Interior design by: Alison Tracey

Library of Congress PCN Data

Rachel Carson / M.M. Eboch
  (Women in Science and Technology)
  ISBN 978-1-73164-326-1 (hard cover)
  ISBN 978-1-73164-290-5 (soft cover)
  ISBN 978-1-73164-358-2 (e-Book)
  ISBN 978-1-73164-390-2 (ePub)
Library of Congress Control Number: 2020945048

Rourke Educational Media
Printed in the United States of America
01-3502011937